SHOUTS OF

Written and Illustrated by:

Rodney M. Pritchard

Shouts of Love

A product of Helmering Publishing LLC
Jefferson City, MO
United States

Written and Illustrated by:
Rodney M. Pritchard

Cover Art Designed by:
James M. Helmering

For Daniel
My greatest inspiration.

Mom and Dad have loved you,
since the day we brought you home.

To hold you tight and keep you safe,

is all we've ever known.

Day by day you grow and grow,

there's so much that you can do.

Even though you may not know,

some things are bad for you.

When Mom or Dad raise their voice,

it's not to make you cry.

There are just some things you must not do,

or say, or even try.

Sometimes you'll get in trouble,
and you won't think its fair.

We only want what's best for you,

and to know how much we care.

So when something is important,

we need you to remember why.

As parents we'd do anything,

to keep it fresh inside your mind.

We never want you to feel,

like we're mean, or that we're mad.

We just love you more than anything,
because we're your Mom and Dad.

THE END

ABOUT THE AUTHOR

Rodney is a dedicated father to his son, Daniel. He lives in a small town in Central Missouri. His love for children's literature began with his first job manufacturing children's books in the state's Capital. He has since then branched out to begin writing his own children's literature using his own daily experiences to reach out to children and their parents. Rodney wrote "Shouts of Love" for his son, Daniel. Rodney wanted to explain to his son how much he loved him, and that as parents, we do sometimes raise our voices, but that doesn't change the immense love and adoration we have for our children. His hope was for other parents to be able to enjoy the book with their children and understand that the tone of our voice may change, but our love never will.

For more great titles visit Helmering Publishing at:
www.helmering.com

www.ingramcontent.com/pod-product-compliance
Lightning Source LLC
Chambersburg PA
CBHW041244040426
42445CB00004B/136

9780692225219